WARREN

Death Waits
AT THE
DEPOT

This book is dedicated to my grandfather, J. D. Robinson, who played a pivotal role in the early history of the little community of Lenox, Georgia, beginning before and continuing after the turn of the twentieth century. This small, close-knit community has been my home for more than seventy years, and I cannot imagine growing up or living anyplace else on earth! It is truly a "Mayberry" USA.

Special thanks go out to Mr. Bryan Shaw of the Berrien County, Georgia Historical Society for his assistance by making research material available for this book. Bryan is a truly devoted historian of Berrien County and has been instrumental in preserving the history and buildings of early Georgia.

Table of Contents

This book is based on a true story that occurred in the frontier of South Georgia in 1909. Two young men from very different backgrounds met for the first time by chance at the railroad depot building in Lenox, Georgia in the early morning hours of April 26th, 1909. Neither man would escape that tragic meeting.

PROLOGUE

Marshall Lewis, Left
Clifford Rutherford, Right

In the early morning hours of April 26th, 1909, two young men, sons of pioneers of the wilderness of South Georgia, were placed together at the same time and place, and although unknown to each other before that fateful day, both names would remain linked to a common tragedy from which neither man would walk away.

Marshall Lewis was a strong, young black man born on June 26th, 1886 in Oakfield, Georgia, located in present day Worth County, to John and Mary Lewis. Oakfield was located near a stagecoach line running from Milledgeville, Georgia, to Tallahassee, Florida. It would later become a depot site for the Albany-Northern Railroad in the late 1890s. The Lewis family raised their ten children to be hard-working, God-fearing Christians, taking them regularly to the Mount Zion Baptist Church in Oakfield. Little else is known about the Lewis family except that they lived in a small sharecropper's home near Oakfield. Marshall grew up there and later would be employed as a hardworking railroad hand. He traveled extensively throughout the southeastern United States and eventually made his way to Eldorado, Georgia, on that fateful day while working for the Georgia Southern and Florida Railway.

Oakfield was a rather prosperous area with a post office, a bank, as well as a mercantile store. The Exchange Bank of Oakfield was chartered by the State of Georgia on November 22, 1911 with capital of $15,000. Mr. John A. Fountain, cashier, was arrested a few years later in Tampa, Florida, and charged with bank embezzlement when it was discovered $15,000 was missing from the bank. The Exchange Bank of Oakfield was subsequently closed, having no capital left. Many depositors lost their money as a result. Mr. Fountain was living in Tampa under the assumed name A. C. Small. He was returned to Sylvester, Georgia, and convicted of embezzlement of between $11,000 and $12,000, was sentenced to six months in jail and twelve months on the chain gang.

Clifford Rutherford was the other central figure in this tragedy of 1909. Clifford was born July 27th, 1883 to Henry and Mary Rutherford in rural Berrien County, Georgia, as one of nine children. Clifford was an ambitious, young, single white man who had just begun a very promising career as assistant postmaster in the new Lenox, Georgia Post Office. With very little other means of communication, the U.S. Post Office represented a vital part of any community and was considered a very prestigious place to be employed. Postal Service jobs were not awarded on a merit basis, but rather were political plums handed out by the party that happened to be in power at the time.

The Georgia Southern & Florida Railroad—sometimes known as the Suwanee River Route, because it crossed over that famous river at White Springs, Florida—opened the new line running from Macon, Georgia, to Palatka, Florida, through the South Georgia frontier in 1888 where Lenox is now located, with plans to extend the route later to include Jacksonville, Florida. The new line boasted 382 miles of track, 34 locomotives, 25 passenger cars, and 1,445 freight cars. A location along the way was chosen by the railroad company as the site for a new depot when it struck a deal with Mr. James D. Kinard, a local resident who donated fifty acres of land in exchange for half interest in the development rights of the new planned community. Having a railroad depot meant prosperity for any area chosen, since it brought commerce with it and availability to far-flung markets. Soon after the opening of the depot, a new town sprang up which had not yet been named. It is said two men were sitting at the depot one day and watched as a farmer drove an ox-drawn cart through town. One man commented to the other, "That man sure is driving a mighty lean ox," which soon gave way to the name Lenox. The first station in Lenox was contained in a railroad boxcar and included a telegraph and express office. Later, in 1891, the Lenox Depot was built on the west side of the railway in the middle of town and was constructed of virgin, long-leaf pine lumber sawed from the logs of nearby ancient timber, probably several hundred years old. The beautiful lumber of this depot remains in use today, and more will be revealed about its fate more than a hundred years later, as its beauty and warmth are still admired and enjoyed.

EARLY GEORGIA

Geographically, Georgia is a very diverse state, with the Appalachian Mountains in the north, joined by the Piedmont section, then the Coastal Plain area that stretches south to the Atlantic Ocean. There is a very distinct separation between the Piedmont and Coastal Plain areas known as the fall line. The fall line marks the area where an ancient sea once splashed on the beach. The coastal plain is the location of this story. After the ocean receded, an enormous region developed that was covered with unbelievably large and beautiful long-leaf pine forests, interspersed with large areas of wiregrass. The logs of these forests were so enormous that they could not be dragged by mule team alone, but required a small tram rail system made of small gauge rails. These were sometimes hauled out by steam driven, miniature engines and sometimes by teams of mules pulling one log at a time over the rails to the sawmills waiting nearby. An enormous volume of lumber was then cut from one log. These forests would probably have been growing when Columbus first visited America. While the region had been blessed with beauty and countless natural resources, it remained largely undeveloped until the middle or latter half of the nineteenth century. A whole new industry developed with the harvesting and distillation of pine sap. This process created a black, sticky, tar that was perfect for waterproofing the bottoms of wooden ships. These enterprises were known as "Naval Stores" for that reason. Also, a clear liquid was produced, known as turpentine, and was good for medicinal purposes as well as other uses. The wire grass provided an abundance of nutritious food for animal life, and was later used by cattlemen who let their cows range freely over these vast plains. There were many rivers and creeks that flowed with pure, clean water, and wildlife such as deer, turkey, quail, and fish were abundant. In years to come, all these natural resources would be useful in the development of this region for generations to come.

The native Americans occupying this area belonged to the Lower Creek Indian tribe. The Creek Indian Nation was divided between at least two tribes. One, the Upper Creeks, lived mostly in Alabama and were the most hostile. The Lower Creeks in South Georgia remained friendly with the white settlers since their treaty with General James Oglethorpe, Georgia's founding father. However, as the 19th century progressed in time, and as the white settlers pressed for more and more land from them, an animosity began to brew between the two cultures. The federal government pressed the Indians to relocate to federal lands in the west—which some did—but most began to flee further south into Florida to join with the Seminole Nation. As the Upper Creeks were forced from Alabama, many chose to travel through south Georgia on their journey to Florida, and many raids and skirmishes with the settlers resulted. The Battle of Brushy Creek in present day Cook County marked the culmination of this animosity. The battle was begun after warriors were first spotted near the intersection of the Warrior Creek and Little River.

All these natural resources were made possible by the hot, humid climate of the region and the unique, rich, sandy, loamy soil. The region remains dominated to this day by agricultural production. As other parts of America began to fully develop, many families began to make their way to south Georgia for various reasons. Some were in search of cheap land for farming, others just for the solitude, while more than a few came to the frontier to escape a shady past and make a new start. A large number of these migrants were of Irish origin who had settled originally in great numbers in North and South Carolina.

One such immigrant family was John and Nancy Ray Robinson, whose heritage reached back to the Shannon River area of Ireland, near present day Ulster. Both were born in Barnwell County of South Carolina, around 1790 to 1800. John and Nancy had three sons, with the youngest being named David Shannon Robinson, in remembrance of their origins from along the Shannon River. One day, John and David Shannon visited a nearby town where the local bully tried to intimidate everyone living in or visiting the area. He spat on young David Shannon in the street, and David's father demanded an apology which was refused, so John challenged the bully to a fight in the middle of town. During the fight that ensued, John struck the bully with a powerful blow to the neck, whereupon the bully fell to the ground and died. Shortly after this incident, John loaded up his family and sparse belongings and headed for the anonymity of the frontier of south Georgia. He made his family's new home in the Cat Creek area of Lowndes County, where he would make a fresh start. He had no intention of waiting around to discover whether he was wanted by the law in South Carolina. Other families would come to the area, leaving their past behind, to take advantage of the opportunities that awaited them. In the early days of the area, travel was limited to a few trails by land and by river navigation. Some of the older trails, which later became established roads, include the Old Union Road, The Coffee Road, and the Old Dixie Highway. It is said that most of these early trails were established by Indians as trading routes to the Gulf or Atlantic coasts seeking salt and sea shells in exchange for furs and corn. The Georgia Legislature acted soon after the turn of the nineteenth century to encourage development of this vast region by awarding land for settlement by the lottery drawing method. The wiregrass region was divided into three large sections, Early, Irwin, and Appling counties. It was ordered that plots of land be surveyed into square plots and numbered, with each containing 490 acres, known as land lots. The land was free, but the recipient was required to pay an administrative fee of $18, which was later reduced to $12 and by 1831 down to just $5. Every free white male was entitled to one draw.

Every white male with a wife and child under twenty-one years of age was entitled to two draws. Revolutionary War veterans were awarded two draws, as well as all widows with children. Orphan families were awarded one draw.

Young Joseph Daniel Robinson

The economy of the area grew steadily and was largely unaffected by the financial crises that arose from an unregulated era of commerce. One dramatic event of the late nineteenth century created a financial boom that was only slowed by the depressions of the early 1900s and, of course, the great depression of the early 1930s. The advent of the Georgia Southern and Florida Railroad would forever change the region. Towns sprang up all along the new line, bringing growth and prosperity to the whole area. Many savvy businessmen saw the opportunities springing forth and soon moved into the region to take advantage. Young Joseph Daniel Robinson, son of David Shannon Robinson, who had moved from the area of Cat Creek to what is now Western Berrien County, Georgia, near Oaky Grove Church, was one of those recognizing the new opportunities. J.D. Robinson proved to be quite an entrepreneur after moving to Lenox. He established a hardware store, was an insurance agent for Woodmen of the World Insurance Society, and owned several farms, including one near town where he established the first dairy operation of the area after purchasing a prize bull at an auction in Madison, Georgia, at the old A&M School. He also acted as a land agent, facilitating land transactions between buyers and sellers of the area.

Before making Lenox his home, Joseph's first job was as principal of the school in Eldorado. The previous principal had been almost literally driven out of town by the wild and undisciplined students, whom he was unable to control. Being made aware of the circumstances,

J. D. decided to get a firm grip on the discipline problem, beginning with the first day of the new school year. After all the students had arrived for the day, J. D. introduced himself and gave a stern lecture as to the consequences of misbehavior. He then instructed them all to line up outside and he proceeded to give an unforgettable demonstration of his prowess with a wooden paddle to each student. They were then dismissed for the day and sent home. There was no need for any further discipline for the rest of the year because they had all learned the lesson of the first day well.

Another enterprising young man of the era was Mr. L. O. Benton of Monticello, Georgia. Benton recognized the need of the new frontier for banking services to help fuel the growth of agriculture and commerce and he soon learned the process for founding new banks in middle Georgia, while making investments in many of the new ventures. Mr. Benton would travel the new railroad and make stops at most of the young communities that had not yet established a bank. One such stop on his travels was at Lenox, Georgia. Benton stayed in the Sears hotel near the Lenox Depot and came to know the community leaders of the day. These included J. D. Robinson, J. L. Brooks, F. B. Vickers, Sim Harrell, J. R. Kinard, and W. H. Clements. Mr. Benton convinced the group that the new community lacked one essential ingredient to further the prosperity of the town: a bank. Benton, having learned the skills necessary to obtain a new bank charter, offered his expertise by doing the required application and paperwork for such a venture in exchange for stock in the new enterprise that he would hold as an investment. It is said this strategy proved to be very profitable for Mr. Benton in years to come.

The Bank of Lenox was thus formed in 1906 with the issuance of $30,000 in capital stock, with J. D. Robinson being the cashier and later the majority shareholder, president, and lender. The original bank office was established in a wooden building previously used by Dr. W. H. Clements and within one year was relocated to the new

Bank exterior as it appeared in 1906, above. Below is the interior of the bank, still in use until the early 1960s.

bank building on East Railroad Street, facing west where the depot was located on the other side of the railway. It was adjacent to the Lenox Post Office, a hardware store, and general dry goods store.

It is reported that one of the bank's customers had recently died and the man's widow, Sally, came to town the following spring to pay a visit at the bank with Mr. Joe, as he was known to most people of the town. After a long visit, Joe asked the widow what he could do for her that day, to which she replied that she had decided to keep the farm she and her husband had farmed for many years, but she needed to borrow $100 to plant the next crop. J. D. replied that he would be pleased to lend her the money, but first he needed to get a "little collateral." Not being very literate or familiar with the jargon of business, Sally looked confused at first, but she soon thought she knew what he wanted. It is said that she looked up at him with a sly grin on her face as she replied, "Why, Mr. Joe, you know I ain't done that kind of thing in years!" Her loan request was promptly approved with no "collateral" being required.

DEATH PAYS A VISIT

April 25th, 1909 dawned on a beautiful spring Sunday, with all the plants and trees putting on tender, new green growth in preparation for the hot summer ahead. Churchgoers all over town were busy putting on their Sunday best before heading out to the Lenox Baptist Church or the Lenox Methodist Church. Wives and mothers had risen early to get the big Sunday meal prepared, which usually included fried chicken, mashed potatoes and gravy, fresh picked turnip greens, along with cornbread or hot buttermilk biscuits and a host of other vegetables. Fresh baked pies and cakes were also a must on any family's menu, with fresh churned butter and milk. The meal was the highlight of the week and often guests were invited to partake, as well as the church pastor, so everything had to be perfect. There were no restaurants and the day was set aside as a day of rest and reverence from a week of long hours of hard work. Local banker J. D. Robinson attended the Lenox Baptist Church, which he helped found since it was more closely attuned to the services he had attended at the Oaky Grove Primitive Baptist Church before moving to Lenox. His wife, Virginia, or Miss Jenny as she was known locally, attended the Lenox Methodist Church, which she helped found and was instrumental in raising the funds for the construction of the church building. Miss Jenny and her two daughters would bake pies and cakes, churn fresh butter, and gather fresh eggs to be sold on the street corner in order to help raise funds for the new church building. The children attended church with Miss Jenny, and consequently most would continue in the Methodist faith the rest of their lives.

Miss Jenny was reared in nearby Adel, Georgia, and was the daughter of James A. Henderson. James was born September 23, 1845 and was buried in the Adel Cemetery on August 10, 1900. James was only sixteen years old when the Civil War broke out, but he enlisted in the Confederate Army and joined a Georgia outfit where he was trained in the use of explosives. After the War, he returned to Adel and established a blacksmith business on the main road through town. His business was just next to the Adel Methodist Church, and a large boardinghouse was located in the same block behind his shop. James noticed someone was stealing wood from his wood stack and he was furious because it required a lot of work to gather the proper logs and split them to be used in his blacksmith furnace. One day, he drilled a small hole in the end of one of the wood sticks and filled it with black gunpowder. Then, he sealed the hole with a mixture of mud and ashes in a way that it became barely noticeable. He knew which stick had the powder in it, but the thief would not know until after he stole it. The next Sunday, while the church was filled with worshipers, the cook at the boardinghouse was busy cooking chicken and dumplings on a wood-fired stove when the church windows rattled and a loud boom was heard coming from the direction of the boardinghouse next door. No one was injured, but it is said the heavy cast-iron stove blasted off the floor and there was chicken and dumplings plastered all over the ceiling. James had found his thief and never had any more wood stolen.

Sunday afternoon was a special time when people often sat on their porch in their favorite rocking chairs or porch swings and welcomed friends, neighbors, and relatives who would drop by unannounced for a friendly visit and to discuss the latest news of the day and often the latest juicy gossip. Families routinely consisted of from eight to ten or more children and they would entertain themselves with games of horseshoes, tug of war, skip the rope, marbles, tree climbing, and jacks. Much laughter and squeals of delight could be heard from the children as the adults sat and talked of adult things.

Six miles north in Eldorado, Marshall Lewis had slept late that day, recovering from a week of hard, exhausting work as part of a railroad section gang. The gang spent long days working with heavy steel rails and wooden crossties, using long crowbars and sledge hammers to repair sections of rail line. They were housed in rail cars parked on a side rail and routinely moved frequently to work on other sections of the line. There was no entertainment except what these men provided for themselves, which often included drinking and gambling, known to them as "skin games." The next day, Monday, April 26th, the hard work would resume.

Clifford Rutherford attended church that morning at nearby Pine Grove Baptist Church with his family, since he was still a single man without a family of his own yet, and also because he still loved his mother's Sunday dinner. Other days of the week, he lived in Lenox, where he worked in the post office and rented a room, most likely at the postmaster's home. Sunday afternoon, he made his way back to Lenox in anticipation of another week at the Lenox Post Office.

Clifford's duties included selling stamps at the front window, sorting incoming mail and placing it in the appropriate mailbox, and presorting outgoing mail, placing it in a large canvas bag that was locked and protected any mail from accidentally spilling out. Twice each day he carried the bag out to the railroad nearby and secured it to a tall metal pole just beside the railway in a way that allowed a passing postal rail car to extend a metal rod from the passing train and grab the bag, which was then pulled inside. Postal clerks hurriedly dumped the contents onto a sorting table inside, and would immediately begin sorting mail for drop off at the next city. Conversely, incoming mail would simply be thrown from the passing mail car in another canvas bag and Clifford would run down the tracks to retrieve the newly delivered mail. A letter addressed to Tifton and dropped off before 10:00 a.m. in Lenox would be in the recipient's Tifton mailbox before noon of the same day. This process has been "streamlined" today so that the same letter takes a total of three or more days to make the thirteen-mile trip.

With few exceptions, everybody would go to bed early for the night since there was no electricity and because they had to rise early, often before sunup, to get necessary chores finished before the new work-day began. Two exceptions this night were Mr. L. A. Sears at his hotel as he sat in a rocking chair on the front porch of the hotel, suffering from insomnia after the death of his newborn child just a week earlier when the child drowned accidentally in a bathtub. From this vantage point, he could easily observe the front entrance of the depot, about thirty yards from his position.

Lenox Depot shown in foreground right, with the Sears Hotel located in the background, right.

Another exception was Marshall Lewis, who had been drinking heavily and was involved in a game of dice among the section crew at Eldorado late that Sunday night, and lost all his money. Marshall, along with two others in the group, decided to make the short six-mile trip, either by foot or using a railroad hand car, down the tracks to Lenox, where they planned to burglarize businesses there, looking for money and more liquor.

Shortly after midnight in what now had become April 26th, 1909, Mr. John Kinard, one of the first settlers in the area and a large landowner, made his way by foot to the front steps of the depot in order to catch the 4:00 a.m. train to Valdosta, thirty-five miles south. Mr. Kinard had extensive land holdings and wanted to arrive as early as possible in order to make an early business appointment there and get back to Lenox before the end of the day. Sitting alone in the dark, Mr. Kinard suddenly noticed a strange light moving about in the post office about forty yards to his left on the east side of the railway. He soon recognized the light to be that of a kerosene lantern and instantly knew something was amiss, so he ran hurriedly to the home nearby where Postmaster Griner and Assistant Postmaster Rutherford were sleeping. He awakened Rutherford immediately and reported what he had just witnessed, and both men rushed toward the scene to investigate. Arriving at the post office, they discovered it had been burglarized along with the adjacent hardware and dry goods store and the Bank of Lenox. All three had apparently been forcefully entered, and a long crowbar, typically used by railroad crews, was found nearby. They continued west across the tracks, probably heading for the home of banker Robinson, when they passed Mr. Sears at his hotel. Mr. Sears reported he had just witnessed three black men rushing toward the depot from the other side of the railroad. All three of the pursuers were armed, and they proceeded to the depot to confront and capture the burglars. Young Rutherford elected to be the first to enter the depot and struck a match as he entered, holding it high above his head in order to gain visibility inside. At that moment, two pistol shots rang out, one striking him in the head above his right eyebrow, the second one grazing his head on the right side. Clifford Rutherford fell to the floor, never to regain consciousness, and died several hours later. Unknown to his pursuers, the assailant was armed with a pistol he had stolen from the bank office nearby that was kept in Robinson's desk drawer. The assailant fled out the door and was fired upon by the two remaining pursuers waiting outside, but he escaped unharmed in the confusion of what had just happened and fled into the night.

THE CHASE BEGINS

News of the tragedy spread rapidly throughout the small community, even under the cover of darkness. Citizens from throughout the area were notified to be on the lookout for the killer as the telegraph agent excitedly notified law enforcement officers in Tifton, Adel, Valdosta, and Nashville, where Berrien County Sheriff I. C. Avera resided. Lenox was located in Berrien County at that time, and Nashville was the county seat of government. Present day Lenox is located in Cook County, with Adel as its county seat, after being formed by an act of the Georgia Legislature in 1917. Many smaller counties were formed out of larger ones in Georgia in the early 1900s to make it possible for citizens of outlying areas to travel to their county seat by horseback in a single day to serve on jury duty and take care of other business.

Officers from nearby towns, including Chief Dampier of Valdosta, arrived early in the day with track dogs, and an organized search was begun. Marshal Mullis in Adel was one of those who had been notified, and he soon discovered the killer hiding in a shanty in Adel's mill quarters. He had suspected the killer had probably fled that way using a railway hand car. Lewis immediately made a full confession of the murder, and the pistol used in the killing

*Adel City Marshal
Mullis*

was still in his possession with two empty chambers. The occupants of the home stated Lewis had confessed the killing to them when he knocked on their door seeking refuge. Lewis was wearing a brand-new suit he had stolen from the general merchandise store in Lenox, where he ditched his old clothing. Within an hour's time after Lewis was captured in Adel and on his way to Nashville, where he would be held by Sheriff Avera in the Berrien County Jail, fifty to one hundred men from Lenox and the surrounding area arrived in Adel with the intention of lynching him. A promise was made that a trial would begin within ten days if the mob would make no further efforts to lynch him. Meanwhile, with Marshall Lewis safely housed in jail, Sheriff Avera arrived back in Nashville with Jim Green in his custody. Green had been captured earlier that day in Lenox and was charged with being an accomplice in the crimes of burglary and murder along with Marshall Lewis. Confirming Mr. Sear's first report after the killing that he had witnessed three negros running toward the depot from the bank, a third suspect was captured in Fender, Georgia, near Eldorado, where he was found hiding inside the commissary of Phillips and Martin that night. It is said this suspect resisted arrest strenuously, requiring several officers to place him in handcuffs. The Fender suspect, along with Jim Green, captured earlier in Lenox, would receive a commitment trial in Nashville a few days later, and it was determined they had only been accomplices to burglary and not to the murder of Clifford Rutherford and should therefore be released.

Upon arriving with Green in Nashville, Sheriff Avera was greeted by a large mob that was very excited and angry and he heard much talk about a lynching. Fearing the worst, Avera enlisted Dr. P. H. Askew to transport him and Lewis to Valdosta, in hopes of housing the prisoner temporarily in the relative safety of the Lowndes County Jail. The trio left Nashville headed for Valdosta, twenty-five miles away, before dark in Dr. Askew's new motor car, the REO Speedwagon, said to be the fastest vehicle in Berrien County, arriving there in the astonishing time of just under two hours, averaging nearly twelve miles per hour! It is reported that Dr. Askew was a portly man and since the Speedwagon was rather small, the three men had a very crowded and uncomfortable ride to Valdosta. The Speedwagon was the product of the REO Motor Car Company founded in 1905 in Lansing, Michigan, by the entrepreneur Ransom E. Olds. Mr. Olds originally founded the Olds Motor Vehicle Company in 1897 and manufactured the Oldsmobile car that he later sold to the General Motors Corporation. After founding his new vehicle company later, he named the new car the "Speedwagon." General Motors Corporation threatened to sue him if the new company or vehicle contained the word "Olds," so instead, he chose to name the new company using his initials, REO. Olds would later begin making a heavy-duty truck that was produced until 1975 and also manufactured buses on the truck platforms. Later in 1968, a new rock and roll band was formed and took the name REO Speedwagon, and became very popular with one of their early hit albums entitled, "You Can Tune a Piano, But You Can't Tuna Fish." The group is still touring the country today performing their memorable tunes.

After arriving in Valdosta and being placed in the custody of Sheriff Passmore of Lowndes County, Lewis had to be transferred a third time when Sheriff Passmore became alarmed after learning an even bigger mob, intent on a lynching, was being formed and would soon be on its way to Valdosta. This time, Lewis was transferred to Savannah, Georgia, where he was held in safekeeping for several days. After being told of the necessity for another transfer, Lewis stated he had no dread of lynching if they would give him enough time in which to pray. He seemed to be very confident of his ability to make peace with God.

Dr. Askew and his Speedwagon

THE TRIAL

Colonel William G. Harrison, Left
Colonel Joseph A. Alexander, Middle
Colonel E. S. Chastain, Right

As tempers began to cool, in a few days, Lewis was returned to confinement in the Berrien County Jail. Circuit Court Judge Robert G. Mitchell of Thomasville was promptly notified and he soon called for a special term of the Grand Jury to be convened in the Nashville Court House. At 10:00 a.m. on a Monday morning in June, the Grand Jury was organized and elected Mr. W. T. Shytle, editor of *The Adel News*, as foreman. The Grand Jury heard testimony from witnesses and returned a murder indictment at 11:38 a.m. The prisoner was brought into court by Solicitor-General W. E. Thomas, and he stated the State of Georgia was ready to proceed. Attorneys for the defendant included Col. Joseph A. Alexander, who was to lead the defense along with William G. Harrison and E. S. Chastain. The defense team consulted with the defendant for a few minutes and announced that they were ready. The noon hour having arrived, the court announced a recess until 1:30 p.m.

Court reconvened as scheduled when the Berrien County Superior Court was called to order by Judge Mitchell. The atmosphere inside the courtroom, and out, would best be described as electric. Reporters from newspapers far and wide were present and eager to record the proceedings for their readers back home. This heinous crime had generated outrage up and down the Atlantic Seaboard and was front page news in newspapers large and small. The courtroom was filled to capacity and included a large number of ladies who were present to hear the proceedings. Large crowds had formed outside the court-house, with some singing hymns, some praying for justice, some for mercy, and others cursing the defendant. Among the jurors selected to hear the evidence were: J. W. Coward, Robert Burns, G. W. Fender, J. W. McKinney, Paul Tyson, J. R. Futch, Z. Spells, and J. E. Golden.

After jury selection was completed, the solicitor began his statement to the jury at 2:40 p.m. and informed them of what he intended to prove. Mr. J. E. Sears of Lenox was called as the first witness put up by the State as an eyewitness to the shooting. He stated he was standing next to Mr. Rutherford when Lewis shot and killed him. He had never seen the negro before or since, but positively identified him as the man who did the shooting. He stated two shots entered Mr. Rutherford's head, one just over the right eye and the other in the edge of the hair. Lewis had entered the depot earlier and when Rutherford and Sears got to the door, Rutherford struck a match to peer inside and was fired upon by Lewis with a .38 caliber Smith & Wesson revolver that had been stolen earlier from the desk drawer of Mr. J. D. Robinson at the Bank of Lenox. Mr. Rutherford died in just two hours. Mr. Sears stated he fired at Lewis as he ran from the depot, but missed his mark. Colonel Alexander cross-examined Mr. Sears but failed to make him deviate from his positive identification of the defendant.

The second witness called to the stand by the State was Mr. J. R. Kinard. He stated he was not an eyewitness to the shooting, but was about fifteen steps away, heard the shots, and saw the negro run out of the depot as Rutherford fell to the floor, mortally wounded. He was the man who first discovered the burglaries and notified Misters Sears, Rutherford, Postmaster Griner, and Lessie Simmons, owner of one of the other buildings that had been burglarized. Kinard also shot at the escaping assailant, but missed his target. Upon cross-examination, he stated that the night was dark, but he was positive Lewis was the man who robbed the stores.

Mr. J. H. Parrish of Adel was the third witness called to testify by the State. He said Lewis was arrested in Adel by Marshal Mullis at 3:00 p.m. the day of the murder in Lenox. He stated that Lewis made a confession in his presence that he shot Mr. Rutherford. A lively tilt ensued between Solicitor Thomas and Lewis' attorneys about the introduction of this confession, but Judge Mitchell ruled that a proper foundation had been laid and it was allowed to go in.

Mr. J. D. Robinson of the Bank of Lenox was the next witness called to the stand, and he testified the pistol placed into evidence was the same pistol he owned and kept in his desk drawer at the bank.

The fifth witness was Mr. J. B. Sirmans. He stated that the clothing worn by the prisoner was from his store in Lenox and had been stolen the night of the murder. Sheriff I. C. Avera was put up next and corroborated Mr. Sirmans' testimony, stating the clothing was the same as that worn by the defendant when he was arrested in Adel.

Railroad agent C. M. McGahee testified that the Express Office in the depot had been robbed the same night, and a pocketknife and some liquor were missing.

The eighth and final witness was Mr. Pleas Carter, a negro who had known Lewis for thirteen years. Lewis was arrested hiding in Carter's shanty at Adel. He stated Lewis told him he had "done some murdering" in Lenox and wanted to hide in his house.

The solicitor announced the State would now close their case. Attorneys for the defense consulted again, after which a recess was taken until 7:30 p.m. The defense for Lewis "closed" without putting up a single witness; neither did the defendant make a single statement to the jury.

After supper, Colonel Alexander announced he had concluded with the examination of the witnesses. Colonels Chastain and Harrison would make the arguments for the defense. Colonel Chastain opened for the defense and made a strong, eighteen-minute plea for mercy. Solicitor Thomas then presented the State's side of the case in a strong argument of one hour. Colonel Harrison next presented to the jury in his usual eloquent style a thirty-three-minute plea on behalf of the defendant.

The judge then delivered a perfect and exhaustive charge to the jury. The jury retired to the jury room, deliberated just eighteen minutes, and brought in a verdict of guilty. The date of execution was set for Friday, July 9th, 1909 at the Berrien County Jail in Nashville.

THE EXECUTION

Death by hanging was the official method of execution in the State of Georgia until 1924, when it was replaced by electrocution. The sheriff of each county was the authorized official in charge, with the responsibility of carrying out the sentence. When the Berrien County Jail was constructed in the early 1900s, it had an execution chamber built into the second floor of the building. The brick jail was built with living quarters on the ground floor where the sheriff and his family resided. It was equipped with a kitchen where the sheriff's wife cooked meals for her family as well as for all the prisoners who were housed upstairs on the second floor.

The second floor had a cell block that could house up to sixteen male prisoners and included one bath area and one toilet. In a separate room, another cell block was equipped to hold up to four female prisoners, who shared one toilet. A third area contained the execution chamber, which had a metal hook installed in the ceiling to which a rope was secured on one end, and the noose on the other. In the floor directly below the hook was a trapdoor where the condemned would stand, with hands tied behind his back. When the sheriff gave the order, the executioner would release the trapdoor and the condemned would fall through to the space below, resulting in a broken neck and death. However, several factors had to be taken into account for a successful execution, such as the condemned man's height and weight, and the rope had to be stretched so that there was no slack when the trapdoor was released. Also, since the ground floor housed the sheriff's living quarters, furniture had to be temporarily moved from underneath the "drop zone."

The railroad passing through Nashville ran east and west just outside the jail on its way to Sparks, Georgia, where it connected with the Georgia Southern & Florida Railway, which ran in a north, south direction.

Though the exact number of executions performed in this location since construction of the jail was completed in the early 1900s is unknown, the last two were certainly memorable. On September 12, 1902, seventeen-year-old Boisy Bryant, a black man, was hanged for the murder of Marshal W. A. Hiers of Adel in May of that year. Marshal Hiers was shot by Bryant when he attempted to arrest him on a misdemeanor charge in Adel. Hiers was shot in the abdomen and lingered in agony for four days before he died. Almost seven years later on the appointed day of July 9, 1909, Marshall Lewis was the last person executed in Berrien County when the trapdoor was released and his body dropped through the space below.

Sheriff Avera stated he had made everything ready, with the gallows in good working order, and the rope had been properly stretched.

On the night before the execution, large crowds gathered around in the town square; some were white, most were black. They sang hymns and prayed loudly, openly weeping and wailing, all while a gentle rain fell and continued throughout the next day. All the ministers in town had visited Lewis several times and prayed with him over the last seven days.

In accordance with the wishes of the Lewis family, the execution was set for 10:00 a.m., or as soon as possible thereafter in order to have time for the body to be loaded onto the 10:40 train to Oakfield, by way of Sparks and Cordele. Marshall's older brother had arrived in town the night before with an order signed by his father for possession of the body for burial in Oakfield. Lewis stated he had made peace with his Maker and was ready and willing to pay the penalty for his crime.

In order to obtain the money to pay for the transport of his body back home to Oakfield, Marshall wrote the following account in his own hand, of his life, and sold it to various newspapers on July 6th, 1909, just days before his execution.

Dear Brethren and Friends:

By way of our Lord and Savior, Jesus Christ, I will try to estimate to you my past life.

I was raised by good parents and all my life was disobedient, and I thought I knew best, but I would not hear what the spirit said but after I received the word of God and was baptized I strayed off in sin and sin is the wages of death, and I believe that a man ought to reap just what he sows.

Now, my dear friends, thy shall not kill, because it will be measured unto you. My brethren, be not many masters, knowing that we shall receive the greater condemnation, for in many things we offend all. If any man will give God his heart, he will be saved. In the city of Nashville, on the 4th day of July, I gave God my heart, and behold, He has made me whole in Jesus name, I will be saved. God is able to make you Holy in His name. Just believe on Him and you will be saved. If God will hear my prayers, he will hear yours, because I have done some of everything but one, that I could think of. Now listen, and Jesus in the name of the Father and Holy Ghost has forgiven me of all my sins. There is not a friend like the lovely Jesus; no not one.

Now my friends I have traveled over the states of Florida, Mississippi, Louisiana, Alabama, Tennessee, Illinois, Kentucky and Georgia, and in all my traveling, I did not learn how to keep out of trouble. I shook hands with a young man in Dyesburg, Tennessee in 1906, and I thought it was a lesson for me. Let me tell you one and all, you can just leave troubles off because it leads to destruction—such as whiskey, pistols and gambling, or anything that will make a man fly into passion; leave it off, because of it there is more trouble in gambling and stealing than anything else.

I remember when I was in Birmingham, I shot a man about twenty-five cents and it was reported that he died. I am not able to tell you everything I have done, as I have done a little of almost everything that I could think of. Now my dear friends this is not to entice you to these wicked things, but I am try-ing to give you a warning that you may be better gentlemen in principles, but you can't have better parents than I had. It is not in our fathers and mothers because they tries with all their hearts to raise us, but sometimes they fail. I was one of those fellows always knew best, but I did not know how close I was to the gallows until a few days ago. If your friends is doing wrong, you must try to stop him and if you can't run with all your might. You must always be mindful—watch and pray. Fighting is a bad thing, I have done so much of it, but I am sorry today that I ever learned how and you will be sorry someday if you take up the habit.

I will ask you with a willing heart and mind to do as your kind parents teach you, for if you have to be hung just like I am going to be, you will wish you had considered what a sweet thing that life is. Therefore don't take that you can't give. Good parents will teach you what is right and wrong, please obey them. Every man must reap what he sows.

Now I will pray and ask God to help you overcome this world of sin, and He will do it. Be careful, be careful; I say any trouble is a bad man.

Now ladies and gentlemen be of good cheer, for I have overcome.

To my best understanding I speak this as a warning to all that they may obey the word of the Lord. My time is most out here, and I want to meet you all again in a happy land where pardon will never be. My heart is sorry for the sins of this world. Let every human call on Jesus. He is able to save you. Whosoever overcomes this world shall wear a long white garment.

May the peace of our Lord and Savior, Jesus Christ,
be with you all,
Amen
In Jesus' Name
Marshall Lewis
Born June 5, 1886
Will die July 9, 1909
Now gentlemen, please, in the name of Jesus, take warning
of this.

At the appointed date and hour, only seventy-two days after brutally murdering twenty-one-year-old Clifford Rutherford in Lenox, Marshall (Doc) Lewis was brought up to the execution chamber at the top of the jail. The rope had been properly tied to the gallows above and extended below where the noose was placed around his neck as his hands were tied behind his back and he stood on top of the trapdoor. With a nod from the sheriff, the executioner released the trapdoor, and Lewis' body fell through the space below.

However, his height and weight were not properly accounted for and the rope stretched slightly, preventing his death, and he remained fully conscious. He was promptly marched back upstairs to the execution chamber, all while blood streamed from his mouth and he begged for water. The rope was adjusted and the trapdoor was again released, resulting in Lewis still not being killed instantly, but dying of strangulation in a few minutes.

Outside the jail moments before execution are: Marshall Lewis, center, Deputy James B. Grimes, left, Sheriff I. C. Avera, right

As a result of the delay in execution, Lewis' body was not ready in time for the final ride back home to Oakfield, Georgia, that day, and his family waited for it to arrive the next day for burial.

Lewis' full public confession and the confession written in his own hand leave no doubt as to his guilt. He admitted to living a life of violent crime and to a second murder of a man over twenty-five cents. However, his written statement also suggests there may have been other killings. The fact that he traveled freely by railroad all over at least seven states presents the real possibility he may have been a serial killer who could commit these acts in one town and simply vanish during the night, only to repeat them far away without ever being noticed.

His admission of sin and repentance, however, along with his public confession of Jesus as his Savior, also suggests he may have died a saved man who was welcomed into Heaven by Jesus Himself!

EPILOGUE

Marshall Lewis' body arrived in Oakfield the following day. It was met at the train depot by his family and carried to the Mount Zion Baptist Church and Cemetery nearby. Besides his family, few people were present as his body was placed in an unmarked grave, and the whereabouts remain unknown to this day.

Clifford Rutherford's funeral, in contrast, was held at Pine Grove Baptist Church near Lenox with a large audience of family, friends, and onlookers as the pastor performed his funeral. His grave is highly visible today, since it is marked with the distinctive tree carved from granite and placed there by the Woodmen of the World Insurance Society. During this era, each life insurance policy issued by Woodmen of the World also included the placement of a fine granite monument. Many of these distinctive monuments can still be found in cemeteries throughout the South.

J. D. Robinson was an agent for Woodmen of the World Insurance Society, and it is entirely possible that since Robinson and Rutherford were from the same area of Berrien County and probably grew up together, J. D. Robinson may have sold the policy to Clifford Rutherford, whose death was a result of a gunshot wound to the head fired from the stolen gun of Mr. Robinson.

*Grave monument honoring Clifford Rutherford
in the Pinegrove Baptist Church Cemetery*

The Lenox Depot continued as the center of commerce in the area for decades to come. It provided affordable passenger transportation that was conveniently located, giving access to almost any destination in the country. It was always busy, loading timber, farm products, and livestock to be sold in faraway markets and brought in mail, coal, and other necessities of daily life. It was also a refueling stop for steam locomotives to take on coal and water. The late 1940s and 1950s witnessed the gradual end of steam-powered engines and the introduction of the diesel-powered locomotive, but transportation in America was on the verge of change.

Mr. Henry Ford began production of the Ford Model T motor car in the early 1900s, but his ingenious use of a "production line" revolutionized that industry and lowered costs to the point that even average working people of America could afford to own one. As Mr. Ford was making his way from Detroit, Michigan, one day down to Miami, Florida, to enter his new automobile in a car show there, he passed through what is now Cook County, Georgia. Near present day Cecil, Georgia, he encountered several swampy places in the cypress ponds of South Georgia and soon bogged his Model T in one of them. Unable to free it himself, he made his way to a nearby farm and politely asked if the famer would lend him a hand and help free his automobile. The farmer willingly hitched up his mule and helped the stranger prepare to be on his way, expecting nothing in return. The stranger handed the farmer a twenty-dollar bill, which was an enormous sum of money in the early 1900s. The farmer asked the man his name so he could remember him. The stranger replied his name was Henry Ford.

The 1950s marked the beginning of another revolution in transportation in the country that changed the railroad industry forever as World War II General Dwight D. Eisenhower became President of the United States and introduced and passed legislation that provided a means of funding for a revolutionary, new, massive transportation system in America called the Interstate Highway System. This system originally consisted of mostly four paved lanes for traffic but has since evolved in size several times. The railroad industry then faced fierce competition for freight traffic from the trucking industry and for passenger traffic from the automobile. Only a small number were able to survive. Adding to the railroad industry's problems was another new means of transportation that also emerged during the mid-twentieth century—air travel. Airplanes revolutionized the movement of passengers and cargo over long distances at great speeds.

In the early twentieth century, the airplane was in its infancy and most people of South Georgia had never seen one. A member of the Godwin family of Lenox related how he and his brothers were hoeing cotton on their daddy's farm one day around 1912. As they were busy at their work, they heard a strange noise in the air above, and they all searched the sky to see what was going on. They had heard the adults talk about a flying machine, but they had never seen one. To them, it was a strange and frightening experience, especially when it began to sputter and backfire, making a loud noise. They watched intently as the sputtering contraption began to descend, and they immediately laid down their tools and began to walk hurriedly toward the place a few miles away where they had observed it disappear from sight.

Other people from far and near had also observed the same incident, and were on their way as well, by foot and muleback, to take a look at the strange machine. The small airplane had experienced engine trouble and made an emergency landing in a field about four miles north of Lenox next to the dirt road now known as Bob Lindsey Rd. There were several tenant houses next to the road that housed farm workers employed to work on the huge 490-acre farm nearby. It was midday, and a grandpa was taking a brief respite from the heat by taking a nap under the shade of a chinaberry tree. As he lay sleeping in his overalls and bare feet, the sputtering plane came down and landed in the field right behind him. The sputtering and backfiring of the engine was so unexpected and frightening, he had a heart attack and died under the chinaberry tree.

The emergence of these revolutionary means of transporting people and cargo created an environment that severely crippled the railroad industry for decades to come. In order to survive, railroad companies responded by cutting costs wherever they could, and they began to close large numbers of depots which were becoming unprofitable to maintain. One such depot sold during the mid-1950s and 1960s was the one in Lenox. The company auctioned off the depot building to the highest bidder, but the purchaser was required to remove it from railroad property. Mr. R. H. Robinson (Roby), son of J. D. Robinson, was the low bidder, purchasing it for $300. He was able to find a moving company that could move the building across the track to a vacant lot nearby that he owned, and used it for many years in the fertilizer and seed company he owned, along with the Bank of Lenox, which he also owned and operated after the death of his father, J. D. Robinson, in 1941.

The Lenox Depot building remained in the Robinson family after Roby's death in 1972 and was leased to the Adel Trading Company as the site of their building and hardware store business in Lenox for many years. It later became vacant and unused. During that same time, a wave of arson swept through the town as someone set fire to several vacant, unoccupied buildings, and the family began to fear the building would fall victim to fire and be lost forever. Later, in the early 1990s, J. D. Robinson's grandson, Warren Robinson, was planning to build a new home with his wife, Margaret, on the fifty-acre farm they owned just north of Lenox on the Bob Lindsey Rd. They struck upon the idea of saving the beautiful old wood of the depot building to be used as flooring in their new home, thus preserving the history of the wood and adding beauty and warmth to their home.

As the depot building was being dismantled to be reworked for its new purpose, the workers discovered a surprise. Lodged in wood near the doorframe of the depot office were two lead bullets. Warren immediately remembered the story he had heard as a child about the murder in 1909 and soon realized these were the two bullets that had been fired from the gun owned by his grandfather, stolen by Marshall Lewis, and used to murder Clifford Rutherford. In addition to the spent shells, an old box containing several unfired bullets has recently surfaced and is believed to be the box of shells used in the killing. The whereabouts of the pistol remains unknown and was last seen at the trial in Nashville. It was most likely held as evidence for a period and later discarded or taken as a souvenir.

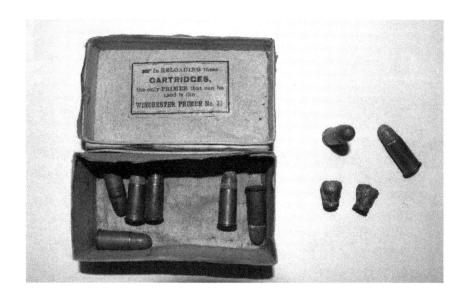

Two spent bullets and box of extra shells, most likely those used to kill Clifford Rutherford.

The Exchange Bank of Oakfield, top and bottom

Clifford Rutherford, upper right, with his family in 1905.

*Inside the old Berrien County Courtroom
with the original bench seats.*

Jury box where twelve jurors sat and decided Marshall Lewis's fate.

Underside of the trapdoor used in the execution.

*Ceiling hook, center, where the execution rope
was attached and stretched below.*

The trapdoor where the prisoner stood just before execution.

Entrance to men's cell block.

Inside men's cell block.

Stairway leading down to the ground floor.

*Outside the jail where Marshall Lewis posed
with the sheriff and deputy sheriff moments before being executed.*

*Outside old Berrien County Jail; the railroad through
Nashville ran where the street is shown to the right.*

*Original Berrien County Courthouse as it stands today,
serving as the home of the Berrien County Historical Society.*

Printed in the USA
CPSIA information can be obtained
at www.ICGtesting.com
LVHW071552210823
755851LV00021B/952